WORLD OF DINOSAURS

AND OTHER PREHISTORIC LIFE

Dougal Dixon

All inquiries should be addressed to:
Barron's Educational Series, Inc.
250 Wireless Blvd.
Hauppauge, New York 11788
www.barronseduc.com

Library of Congress Control Number: 2008925398

ISBN-13: 978-0-7641-4082-2

Printed by CCSZ in China, November 2013
9 8 7 6 5 4

Picture credits (t=top; b=bottom; c=center; l=left; r=right):
Main illustrations:
Lisa Anderson: 32-33.
Simon Mendez: 1, 10-11, 18-19, 22-23, 24-25, 26-27, 50-51, 54-55, 66-67 76-77, 78-79, 82-83, 86-87, 94-95, 98-99, 100-101, 102-103, 106-107.
Bob Nicholls: 44-45.
Luis Rey: 2, 6-7, 36-37, 39-39, 40-41, 42-43, 46-47, 48-49, 52-53, 56-57, 58-59, 60-61, 62-63, 64-65, 68-69, 70-71, 72-73, 74-75 84-85.
Chris Tomlin: 8-9, 12-13, 14-15, 16-17, 20-21, 28-29, 30-31, 34-35,80-81, 88-89, 90-91, 92-93, 96-97, 104-105.
Further Images:
Hu Lan/Alamy: 14. Mervyn Rees/Alamy: 19. Lisa Alderson: 5 (Mesozoic Era bottom). Amherst College Museum of Natural History: 78. Louie Psihoyos/Corbis: 53. The Field Museum: 71.
Gondwana Studios: 63. Simon Mendez: 5 (Mesozoic Era top, Paleozoic Era top), 17. The Natural History Museum, London: 48, 81 106. Luis Rey: 5 (Mesozoic Era centre, Paleozoic Era bottom).
Ria Novosti/Science Photo Library: 82. Tyler Olson/Shutterstock: 57. Shutterstock: 93. Chris Tomlin: 20, 31.
Ticktock Media Archive: 4TL, 4TR, 5 (Cenozoic Era), 6, 8, 11, 13, 22, 25, 27, 29, 32, 35, 37, 39, 41, 43, 45, 46, 50, 54, 59, 61, 64, 67, 68, 75, 76, 85, 86, 89, 91, 95, 98, 101, 103, 104.

CONTENTS

INTRODUCTION

This map shows how Earth looked at the end of the Paleozoic Era. Most of Earth's continents are grouped into one mass of land.

This map shows how Earth looks today. See how different it is! The continents have split up and moved around.

This book tells the story of the development of animals on Earth – from the first shelled creatures to mammals. Earth's history is divided into sections called eras, which are then divided into periods. Each period lasted for millions of years.

The chapters in this book look at the most exciting animals from each prehistoric period. The chapters are color-coded to match the timeline on page 5.

Each animal has its own factfile, providing information on the era it lived in, its habitat, its size, the food it ate, its predators, and amazing fossil finds.

PREHISTORIC WORLD TIMELINE

Use this timeline to trace prehistoric life. It shows how simple creatures developed into many different kinds of animals. This took millions and millions of years. That is what MYA stands for – millions of years ago.

		PERIOD	
CENOZOIC ERA	**ICE AGE**	1.75 MYA to now QUATERNARY	This is a period of ice ages and mammals. Our direct relatives, Homo sapiens, also appear.
	ANCIENT MAMMALS	65 to 1.75 MYA TERTIARY	Giant mammals and huge, hunting birds appear in this period. Our first human relatives also start to develop.
MESOZOIC ERA	**CRETACEOUS LIFE**	135 to 65 MYA CRETACEOUS	Huge dinosaurs develop. They have all died by the end of this period.
	JURASSIC LIFE	203 to 135 MYA JURASSIC	Large and small dinosaurs and flying creatures develop.
	TRIASSIC LIFE	250 to 203 MYA TRIASSIC	The "Age of Dinosaurs" begins. Mammals also start to appear.
PALEOZOIC ERA	**EARLY LIFE**	295 to 250 MYA PERMIAN	Sail-backed reptiles start to appear.
		355 to 295 MYA CARBONIFEROUS	The first reptiles appear, and tropical forests develop.
		410 to 355 MYA DEVONIAN	Bony fish develop. Trees and insects appear.
		435 to 410 MYA SILURIAN	Fish with jaws develop, and land creatures appear.
		500 to 435 MYA ORDOVICIAN	Primitive fishes, trilobites, shellfish, and plants develop.
		540 to 500 MYA CAMBRIAN	First animals with skeletons appear.

PARADOXIDES

Paradoxides belonged to a group of animals called the trilobites. These were the most important sea-living animals of the Cambrian Period. There were no land-living animals at this time. Trilobites were covered in a shell made of material similar to your nails. They also had jointed legs. Shrimps have similar shells.

There were thousands of different kinds of trilobites. They all had a big head shield and a tail shield, and the body in between consisted of movable segments. Some trilobites could swim, some could burrow, and others could roll up into a ball.

ANIMAL
FACTFILE

NAME: *Paradoxides* (like a puzzle)

PRONOUNCED: par-oh-dox-ee-dees

GROUP: Trilobite

WHERE IT LIVED: Canada, Europe, North Africa

WHEN IT LIVED: Early to middle Cambrian Period (570 to 517 million years ago)

LENGTH: 10 inches (25 cm)

SPECIAL FEATURES: Spines at the edge of each body segment

FOOD: Particles on the seabed

MAIN ENEMY: Big arthropods

DID YOU KNOW?: *Paradoxides* was one of the first trilobites to develop.

Paradoxides (on the right of this picture) was one of the biggest trilobites. It was hunted by even bigger animals, like the fearsome *Anomalocaris* that you see here.

DIPLOGRAPTUS

In the surface waters of early Paleozoic times lived tiny creatures that looked like jellyfish. They were called graptolites. The *Diplograptus* you see here were a type of graptolite. They had two rows of cups back to back. Each cup contained an animal. The cups were attached to a unit shaped like a UFO. This is called a float. Graptolite colonies floated through the oceans anchored to their floats.

A graptolite colony looked like the blade of a saw. Each "tooth" was a tiny cup that held an individual animal. Colonies consisted of dozens of these individuals attached together.

ANIMAL
FACTFILE

NAME: *Diplograptus* (double graptolite)

PRONOUNCED: dip-low-grap-tus

GROUP: Graptolite

WHERE IT LIVED: Worldwide, in all the oceans

WHEN IT LIVED: Late Ordovician Period (443 to 439 million years ago)

LENGTH: each string was about 4 inches (10 cm)

SPECIAL FEATURES: Two rows of cups back to back

FOOD: Floating organic matter

MAIN ENEMY: None

DID YOU KNOW?: Other graptolite colonies have names based on how the cups were arranged. *Monograptus* had a single row of cups, *Tetragraptus* had four rows of cups, *Didymograptus* had two separate rows.

Each tiny graptolite organism in the colony had a feathery feeding organ that trailed in the water. These gathered floating food particles.

CEPHALASPIS

Fish developed at the beginning of the Paleozoic Era. The first fish, like *Cephalaspis*, had no jaws, just a sucker for a mouth. *Cephalaspis* did not have much of a skeleton either – just a backbone and a skull. Its head was protected by an armored shield, like that of a trilobite.

Cephalaspis fed from the bottom of streams and lakes. The fin on the underside of its tail kept the head downward, and the sucker mouth could sift for food in the sand of the bed.

These fossil fish were the earliest of the vertebrates – the animals with backbones.

ANIMAL FACTFILE

NAME: *Cephalaspis* (head-shield fish)

PRONOUNCED: sef-al-as-pis

GROUP: Agnatha – the jawless fish

WHERE IT LIVED: Freshwater in Northern Europe

WHEN IT LIVED: Devonian Period (408 to 362 million years ago)

LENGTH: Close to 5 inches (12 cm)

SPECIAL FEATURES: *Cephalaspis* may have had electric organs on its head. They would have given an electric shock to any predator that tried to attack.

FOOD: Organic scraps on the river bed

MAIN ENEMY: Big arthropods like giant scorpions

DID YOU KNOW?: It was from little fish like this that the whole range of modern backboned animals developed.

TIKTAALIK

Among the fish of the Devonian Period, there were a few that might have been able to spend some time out of the water. These had lungs and were able to breathe air. They would not have been able to spend much time on land, but they were the first backboned animals to do so. *Tiktaalik* was likely one of these.

Tiktaalik had bony fins. These had a shoulder, elbow, and wrist. This means the fins worked a bit like legs. The skull was more like a crocodile's than that of a fish.

ANIMAL
FACTFILE

NAME: *Tiktaalik* (a native word for a big fish)

PRONOUNCED: tik-ta-lick

GROUP: Crossopterygian — with fins that could move them on land or in the water

WHERE IT LIVED: Northern Canada

WHEN IT LIVED: Late Devonian Period (375 million years ago)

LENGTH: 9 feet (2.7 meters)

SPECIAL FEATURES: Two pairs of fins that acted like legs, and lungs that allowed it to breathe on land.

FOOD: Small fish or arthropods

MAIN ENEMY: Bigger fish

DID YOU KNOW?: There are fish today, such as the mudskipper of the tropics, that can spend time on land.

Tiktaalik lived in streams and ponds. When these dried up in hot weather, it might have been able to use its ability to crawl over land to find new ponds in which to live.

13

ICHTHYOSTEGA

Ichthyostega is one of the earliest amphibians that we know about. Although it had the body, legs, and toes of a land-living animal, it had the head of a fish and a fishy fin on the tail. This shows that its ancestors were fish.

Ichthyostega probably had a lifestyle quite similar to the mudskipper, found in tropical regions today. Mudskippers are fish, but they have special adaptations that allow them to spend time on land.

ANIMAL
FACTFILE

NAME: *Ichthyostega* (fish skull)

PRONOUNCED: ick-thee-oh-stay-ga

GROUP: Labyrinthodon –
the earliest amphibians

WHERE IT LIVED: Greenland

WHEN IT LIVED: Late Devonian
Period (377 – 362 million years ago)

LENGTH: 3 feet (1 meter)

SPECIAL FEATURES: Strong shoulders
and hips, to work the legs and feet

FOOD: Insects and other small animals

MAIN ENEMY: Big fish

DID YOU KNOW?: A strange thing
about *Ichthyostega* is the number of
its toes. It had eight toes on the hind
foot and six on the front. Later
backboned animals would have a
maximum of five toes on each foot.

Even though it was possibly
adapted to living on land,
Ichthyostega probably spent
most of its time in the
water. Its feet helped it
push its way through
thick water weeds.

15

WESTLOTHIANA

The big difference between amphibians and reptiles is the fact that reptiles can lay their eggs on land. While amphibians need to lay their eggs in water, *Westlothiana* was probably able to lay its eggs on land. This, plus its age, would make it the oldest known reptile.

Westlothiana looked just like a little lizard. It probably lived like one too, chasing insects through the undergrowth.

Only one fossil of *Westlothiana* has been found, and that was in a quarry where there were also fossils of spiders, scorpions, and land plants. They all lived together in swampy forests.

ANIMAL FACTFILE

NAME: *Westlothiana* (from West Lothian, the county in Scotland where it was found)

PRONOUNCED: west-low-thee-ah-na

GROUP: Possibly a very early reptile

WHERE IT LIVED: Scotland

WHEN IT LIVED: Early Carboniferous Period (338 million years ago)

LENGTH: 1 foot (30 cm)

SPECIAL FEATURES: Ability to lay eggs and live on land full time

FOOD: Insects and spiders

MAIN ENEMY: *Brontoscorpio*, a giant scorpion about 3.3 feet (1 meter) long

DID YOU KNOW?: Although we think *Westlothiana* was a reptile, its skeleton is very similar to that of an amphibian. *Westlothiana* shows how reptiles developed from amphibians.

DIMETRODON

The Permian Period was the last period of the Paleozoic Era. When it began, deserts covered most of Earth. *Dimetrodon* was a reptile that was well adapted to living in the hot, dry conditions.

In the cold desert mornings *Dimetrodon* could hold up the sail on its back to the Sun, to warm itself. In the heat of the day, wind passing over the sail would cool it down.

Dimetrodon had two types of teeth. This is unusual for a reptile. It had long teeth in front to cut through meat, and short ones behind to tear it into small pieces.

ANIMAL
FACTFILE

NAME: *Dimetrodon* (two kinds of teeth)

PRONOUNCED: di-met-ro-don

GROUP: Pelycosaur

WHERE IT LIVED: Texas

WHEN IT LIVED: Early Permian Period (290 to 256 million years ago)

LENGTH: 11 feet (3.3 meters)

SPECIAL FEATURES: Tall spines covered by skin, forming a sail on its back

FOOD: Other reptiles

MAIN ENEMY: None

DID YOU KNOW?: Many people wrongly think that *Dimetrodon* was a dinosaur. It lived a long time before the dinosaurs and was not closely related at all.

YCAENOPS

Lycaenops had a long skull with sharp teeth and long legs for running fast. It may have lived in packs. Many scientists think it looked and behaved rather like a wolf. Permian reptiles like *Lycaenops* were the distant ancestors of the mammals.

Lycaenops had killing teeth at the front of its mouth, and meat-shredding teeth at the back. Modern wolves use their teeth in the same way.

ANIMAL
FACTFILE

NAME: *Lycaenops* (looking like a dog)

PRONOUNCED: lie-kee-nops

GROUP: Gorgonopsian — one of the groups of mammal-like reptiles

WHERE IT LIVED: South Africa

WHEN IT LIVED: Late Permian Period (256 to 245 million years ago)

LENGTH: 3 feet (1 meter)

SPECIAL FEATURES: Dog-like or wolf-like teeth

FOOD: Other reptiles

MAIN ENEMY: Bigger meat-eating reptiles

DID YOU KNOW?: *Lycaenops* had legs close to its body (like mammals today) not out to the side (like a crocodile's legs). This helped it to run faster than the other animals of the time.

There were bigger hunting reptiles around at the time, but *Lycaenops* would have been a fierce predator of smaller reptiles.

SEPHODERMA

By the time of the Triassic Period, there were all kinds of animals living on land. There were also many that returned to the sea and found it easier to live there. The placodonts were a group of reptiles that lived in the sea and ate shellfish. *Psephoderma* had a long, pointed snout and strong jaws. It was ideally adapted for picking shellfish off reefs and crushing them with its broad teeth.

Psephoderma

Psephoderma had
a shell on its back
and looked rather like a turtle.
You can see the shell in this fossil.
However, *Psephoderma* was not closely related to
the turtles. It developed a similar shape and shell
because it had a similar lifestyle.

Placochelys

22

Henodus

ANIMAL FACTFILE

NAME: *Psephoderma* (rough skin)

PRONOUNCED: sef-oh-der-ma

GROUP: Placodont – a group of swimming shellfish-eaters

WHERE IT LIVED: The seas around Southern Europe

WHEN IT LIVED: Late Triassic Period (223 to 209 million years ago)

LENGTH: 5 feet (1.5 meters)

SPECIAL FEATURES: Turtle-like shell on the back and another over the hips

FOOD: Shellfish

MAIN ENEMY: Other big swimming reptiles and shark-like fish

DID YOU KNOW?: Not all placodonts had shells. Some looked like giant newts. One relative, *Placodus*, was 6.5 feet (2 meters) long.

The placodonts in this picture all had armored backs. Their shells would have protected them from the other sea-living reptiles of the time – some of which were much larger and fiercer.

OTHOSAURUS

Nothosaurus was one of the earliest sea-living reptilian hunters. Its feet were webbed, like those of a seal, and it had quite a long neck and long toothy jaws – just right for snatching at fish. It had a long tail to help it to swim. Even though *Nothosaurus* spent most of its time in the water, it had to come to the surface to breathe.

Ceresiosaurus

There were several types of nothosaur. *Lariosaurus* was one of the smallest, about 24 inches (60 cm) long. *Ceresiosaurus* and *Nothosaurus* were bigger and adapted better to life in the sea. They had long necks that made it easier to catch fish and feet that were used like paddles.

Lariosaurus

Nothosaurus

Fossils of nothosaurs – the group to which *Nothosaurus* belonged – have been found all over the world. *Nothosaurus* was the most common and widespread of them.

ANIMAL FACTFILE

NAME: *Nothosaurus* (false lizard)

PRONOUNCED: noth-oh-sawr-us

GROUP: Nothosaur

WHERE IT LIVED: From Europe and North Africa to China

WHEN IT LIVED: The whole of the Triassic Period (245 to 208 million years ago)

LENGTH: 10 feet (3 meters)

SPECIAL FEATURES: Webbed feet and long sharp teeth

FOOD: Fish and smaller swimming reptiles

MAIN ENEMY: Sharks

DID YOU KNOW?: *Nothosaurus* did not spend all of its time at sea. The bones of its legs show that it was capable of clambering about on land. It would have likely needed to come ashore in order to lay eggs.

SHONISAURUS

Among the reptiles that returned to the sea, probably the most famous are the ichthyosaurs – the "fish-lizards." These were so well adapted to living in the sea that they could not have spent any time on land. Some of the earliest forms, like *Shonisaurus*, were truly enormous – truly whale-sized.

Shonisaurus was the biggest sea animal of the Triassic Period. One species, *Shonisaurus sikanniensis*, was 69 feet (21 meters) long. Its fossil was found in a remote river bank in Canada.

ANIMAL
FACTFILE

NAME: *Shonisaurus* (lizard from the Shoshone Mountains, Nevada)

PRONOUNCED: shon-ee-sawr-us

GROUP: Ichthyosaur — the "fish-lizards"

WHERE IT LIVED: The sea that covered parts of the U.S. and Canada in Triassic times

WHEN IT LIVED: Late Triassic Period (235 to 223 million years ago)

LENGTH: 50 feet (15 meters)

SPECIAL FEATURES: Its size! It was the biggest ichthyosaur known

FOOD: Fish and sea-going invertebrates, like ammonites

MAIN ENEMY: None

DID YOU KNOW?: Scientists think that *Shonisaurus* only had teeth when it was young. Adults were toothless.

This fossil shows a typical ichthyosaur. These reptiles were strong swimmers with streamlined bodies that enabled them to slide effortlessly through the water. The large paddles were actually fingers that had become joined together.

EUDIMORPHODON

Toward the end of the Triassic Period,
the reptiles mastered the skill of
flying. Until then there had
been a few lizard-like reptiles
that were able to glide for
long distances. But now the
pterosaurs appeared – reptiles that
could fly by flapping their wings
like birds. *Eudimorphodon* was one
of the first of the pterosaurs.

The pointed front teeth of *Eudimorphodon* were ideal
for catching fish as it flew low over the
surface of quiet lagoons. The smaller
teeth at the back of the mouth
would have gripped the slippery prey firmly
while it was taken back to land to be eaten.

Like other pterosaurs, *Eudimorphodon* had wings that were supported by a single, long fourth finger. It also had a long, stiff tail that it used for steering.

ANIMAL FACTFILE

NAME: *Eudimorphodon* (with two very differently shaped teeth)

PRONOUNCED: you-dee-morf-oh-don

GROUP: Pterosaur — the flying reptiles

WHERE IT LIVED: Italy

WHEN IT LIVED: Late Triassic Period (235 to 208 million years ago)

BODY LENGTH: 2 feet (0.6 meters)

WINGSPAN: 3.3 feet (1 meter)

SPECIAL FEATURES: Two different types of teeth

FOOD: Fish

MAIN ENEMY: Big fish and big reptiles

DID YOU KNOW?: One fossil of a close relative, *Preondactylus*, was found as a bundle of bones coughed up by a fish that had eaten it over 200 million years ago.

ARIZONASAURUS

The fiercest meat-eaters in Triassic times were big, land-living crocodiles like *Arizonasaurus*. They did not sprawl, like modern crocodiles, but walked on straight legs, like dogs. They prowled around the desert landscapes hunting the big plant-eating reptiles that lived in the oases of the time.

The sail may have kept *Arizonasaurus* warm, by taking in heat from the sun in the chilly mornings. This would have made it more active than its slow-moving prey, and would have helped it to hunt.

The first fossils of *Arizonasaurus* were found in 1947, but the scientists of the time thought they were just dinosaur bones. It was not until 2000 that it was realized the fossils came from a type of crocodile, not a dinosaur. The new animal was named *Arizonasaurus*.

ANIMAL FACTFILE

NAME: *Arizonasaurus* (lizard from Arizona)

PRONOUNCED: a-riz-oh-na-sawr-us

GROUP: Rauisuchian — a group of land-living crocodiles

WHERE IT LIVED: Arizona

WHEN IT LIVED: Middle Triassic Period (240 to 230 million years ago)

LENGTH: 10 feet (3 meters)

SPECIAL FEATURES: Tall sail on its back

FOOD: Plant-eating reptiles

MAIN ENEMY: Bigger, land-living crocodiles

DID YOU KNOW?: *Arizonasaurus* looked rather like *Dimetrodon*, an earlier reptile with a sail on its back. In fact, these two reptiles are not closely related. They look the same because their lifestyles were similar.

EORAPTOR

In late Triassic times, many of the big land animals were crocodile relatives and other reptiles. The first dinosaurs were really quite small. *Eoraptor* was only the size of a fox, but it was an ancestor of the huge and magnificent dinosaurs to come.

This copy of an *Eoraptor* skull shows its long jaws and sharp teeth, just like those of later meat-eating dinosaurs. *Eoraptor* was also the same general shape as later predators. Its small body was carried on two strong hind legs. The arms were smaller with grasping fingers, and its neck was long and flexible. A long, heavy tail helped the dinosaur to balance.

ANIMAL
FACTFILE

NAME: *Eoraptor* (early hunter)

PRONOUNCED: ee-oh-rap-tor

GROUP: Theropod dinosaur

WHERE IT LIVED: Patagonia in South America

WHEN IT LIVED: Late Triassic Period (228 million years ago)

LENGTH: 3.3 feet (1 meter)

SPECIAL FEATURES: The earliest dinosaur known

FOOD: Small animals and insects

MAIN ENEMY: Big, land-living crocodiles

DID YOU KNOW?: Later meat-eating dinosaurs had three, or even two, fingers on the hand. Like its ancestors, *Eoraptor* still had five, although two of them were tiny. Changes like this help scientists to trace the development of dinosaurs.

Although *Eoraptor* was not very big, it was very active and fierce. It hunted small creatures of the time, such as reptiles and insects.

UNAYSAURUS

Dinosaurs quickly developed into two groups: the meat-eaters and the plant-eaters. *Unaysaurus* was one of the earliest of the plant-eating groups. Like other dinosaurs of the time, *Unaysaurus* was smaller than many other animals around. Its later descendants were much bigger – they were the massive, long-necked sauropods such as *Brachiosaurus*.

Unaysaurus had teeth that were roughly serrated, like vegetable graters. It ate plants that grew on the ground and probably also stood on its hind legs, to reach leaves high up in trees.

Part of the *Unaysaurus* skeleton found in Brazil in 2004. From this, scientists can see that the hind legs of *Unaysaurus* were much longer and heavier than its front legs. This suggests that it was able to spend a lot of time on its hind legs.

ANIMAL FACTFILE

NAME: *Unaysaurus* (Black Water lizard, named after the area where it was found)

PRONOUNCED: you-na-sawr-us

GROUP: Prosauropod dinosaur

WHERE IT LIVED: Brazil

WHEN IT LIVED: Late Triassic Period (225 to 200 million years ago)

LENGTH: 7.9 feet (2.4 meters)

SPECIAL FEATURES: The earliest known of the long-necked plant-eaters

FOOD: Leaves and ferns

MAIN ENEMY: Big, land-living crocodiles and early dinosaurs

DID YOU KNOW?: *Unaysaurus* was closely related to other dinosaurs found in North America, Germany and China. This shows the same kinds of animals lived all over the world at that time.

COELOPHYSIS

The early meat-eating dinosaurs may have been small, but some of them made up for this in cunning. *Coelophysis* was one of the earliest of the meat-eaters. There is evidence that it hunted in packs. Pack-hunting animals can successfully hunt beasts much larger than themselves.

Coelophysis was probably a scavenger as well as a hunter, and ate almost anything it could find. Many types of fish and reptiles have been found in its stomach.

Two forms of *Coelophysis* fossil have been found. One form is thinner and more delicate than the other. It is thought they are male and female dinosaurs.

ANIMAL
FACTFILE

NAME: *Coelophysis* (hollow form)

PRONOUNCED: see-low-fye-sis

GROUP: Theropod dinosaur

WHERE IT LIVED: Arizona and New Mexico

WHEN IT LIVED: Late Triassic Period (225 to 220 million years ago)

LENGTH: 10 feet (3 meters) — but most was neck and tail, and its body was about the same size as a fox

SPECIAL FEATURES: Lived and hunted in packs

FOOD: Other reptiles

MAIN ENEMY: Big, land-living crocodiles

DID YOU KNOW?: A fossil skull of *Coelophysis* was taken on the space shuttle *Endeavor* in 1998. It was the first dinosaur in space!

CYNOGNATHUS

One group of reptiles became very similar to mammals in Triassic times. They were probably warm-blooded, like mammals, and had a similar body shape. They might have even had fur. Eventually this group developed into the mammals themselves, in the Triassic Period. *Cynognathus* was one of the most mammal-like of these reptiles.

Scientists think *Cynognathus* was covered in fur because the bones of its snout show tiny pits where whiskers would have been. Only furry animals have whiskers.

The skull of the *Cynognathus* is very similar to the skull of a mammal. Only the shape of the jaw shows that it was actually a reptile.

ANIMAL FACTFILE

NAME: *Cynognathus* (dog jaw)

PRONOUNCED: sy-nog-nay-thus

GROUP: Therapsid group of mammal-like reptiles

WHERE IT LIVED: South Africa

WHEN IT LIVED: Middle Triassic Period (245 to 230 million years ago)

LENGTH: 5 feet (1.5 meters)

SPECIAL FEATURES: Teeth like a dog, with nipping incisors at the front, stabbing canines at the side, and meat-shearing molars at the back

FOOD: Other animals

MAIN ENEMY: The big, land-living crocodiles

DID YOU KNOW?: The jawbone of *Cynognathus*, or something closely related, has been found in Antarctica. This shows that Africa and Antarctica were jointed together in Triassic times.

*I*CHTHYOSAURUS

In the Mesozoic Era, the seas were full of swimming reptiles. One of the most common were the ichthyosaurs, or "fish-lizards." When they first developed, ichthyosaurs were big whale-like animals. By the time of the Jurassic Period, the ichthyosaurs, including *Ichthyosaurus* itself, were smaller and more dolphin-like.

Ichthyosaurs gave birth to live young. They did not need to come ashore to lay eggs. We know this because there are fossils of baby ichthyosaurs preserved while actually emerging from their mother's body.

Ichthyosaurus and the other ichthyosaurs were the fastest hunters in the Jurassic seas. Like modern dolphins they could chase and catch the fastest of the fish and squid-like animals that lived at the time.

ANIMAL
FACTFILE

NAME: *Ichthyosaurus* (fish lizard)

PRONOUNCED: ik-thee-oh-sawr-us

GROUP: Ichthyosaur

WHERE IT LIVED: Worldwide

WHEN IT LIVED: Early Jurassic period (208 to 178 million years ago)

LENGTH: 7 feet (2 meters)

SPECIAL FEATURES: Most streamlined and fish-like of the reptiles

FOOD: Fish and cephalopods

MAIN ENEMY: Pliosaurs

DID YOU KNOW?: Usually we do not know what the soft fleshy parts of a fossil animal look like, but some fossils of *Ichthyosaurus* still have their fins preserved.

CRYPTOCLIDUS

The plesiosaurs were one of the most important swimming reptiles of Jurassic times. There were two types – those with long necks and those with short necks. *Cryptoclidus* was a long-necked plesiosaur.

"Like a snake threaded through a turtle" was the description of a long-necked plesiosaur given by one early paleontologist. The long neck, the broad body, and the paddles give this impression.

Cryptoclidus moved through the water with a flying action, with the front paddles working like wings, and the hind paddles as stabilizers. It could reach around for food with its long neck.

ANIMAL
FACTFILE

NAME: *Cryptoclidus* (hidden collar bone)

PRONOUNCED: crip-tow-cly-dus

GROUP: Long-necked plesiosaurs

WHERE IT LIVED: Europe

WHEN IT LIVED: Late Jurassic Period (165 to 150 million years ago)

LENGTH: 26 feet (8 meters)

SPECIAL FEATURES: Long pointed teeth ideal for catching slippery prey

FOOD: Fish and squid

MAIN ENEMY: Short-necked plesiosaurs, such as *Liopleurodon*

DID YOU KNOW?: Fossils form more easily in the sea than on land, so fossils from swimming reptiles are more common than fossils from some land animals. Scientists were studying plesiosaur fossils long before they disovered dinosaur fossils.

LIOPLEURODON

The biggest reptiles of the Jurassic seas, and probably the biggest meat-eating animals of all time, were the pliosaurs. They had short necks and very long jaws. The biggest of these was the huge *Liopleurodon*.

Liopleurodon could adjust its buoyancy in the water by swallowing or spitting out stones. Its streamlined body meant that, despite its size, it could swim as fast as any other sea reptile of the time. Its head was big enough to swallow you whole had you been around. What a monster!

ANIMAL
FACTFILE

NAME: *Liopleurodon* (smooth-sided tooth)

PRONOUNCED: lie-oh-ploor-oh-don

GROUP: Short-necked plesiosaurs

WHERE IT LIVED: Northern Europe

WHEN IT LIVED: Late Jurassic Period (165 to 150 million years ago)

LENGTH: 50 feet (15 meters)

SPECIAL FEATURES: Possibly the biggest sea reptile of the time

FOOD: Other sea reptiles

MAIN ENEMY: None

DID YOU KNOW?: Short-necked plesiosaurs ranged in size from penguin-sized to the size of a sperm whale. *Liopleurodon* was one of the biggest.

This is the tooth of a *Liopleurodon*. It is about 8 inches (20 cm) long. Bite marks from *Liopleurodon* have been found on the bones of ichthyosaurs and other plesiosaurs, showing that *Liopleurodon* was a fearsome predator.

45

PTERODACTYLUS

The skies were full of flying animals in late Jurassic times, including insects and the first birds. However, the most important flying animals were reptiles, the pterosaurs. There were two groups, the long-tailed pterosaurs and the short-tailed pterosaurs. *Pterodactylus* was a short-tailed pterosaur.

Many well-preserved pterosaur fossils have been found. Here you can clearly see the bones of the spine and neck. In some fossils, it is even possible to see the wing membrane.

ANIMAL
FACTFILE

NAME: *Pterodactylus* (wing finger)

PRONOUNCED: ter-oh-dak-til-us

GROUP: Pterodactyloid – the short-tailed pterosaurs

WHERE IT LIVED: Northern Europe and Africa

WHEN IT LIVED: Late Jurassic Period (157 to 146 million years ago)

WINGSPAN: 3 feet (1 meter)

SPECIAL FEATURES: Broad wings, a short tail and a long neck

FOOD: Fish and small reptiles

MAIN ENEMY: Larger pterosaurs

DID YOU KNOW?: The first pterosaurs found were thought to have been swimming animals – scientists thought that the wings were fins.

The common name "pterodactyl" is used for the whole of the pterosaur group. Scientifically, though, it should only be used for the *Pterodactylus* group. There were many different sizes and shapes of pterosaur at that time.

ETERODONTOSAURUS

Look at this! Big fierce teeth. Grasping claws. Aggressive pose. It must be a ferocious meat-eater! Wrong. *Heterodontosaurus* was a plant-eating dinosaur that probably scared away its enemies by putting on a show. If that did not work, it was small and light enough to run away quickly.

This skull of *Heterodontosaurus* is one of the best-preserved fossil dinosaur skulls known. It was found in South Africa in 1966. The complete skeleton of *Heterodontosaurus* shows that it had long running hind legs, and its short arms had little hands for grasping.

ANIMAL
FACTFILE

NAME: *Heterodontosaurus* (lizard with differently-shaped teeth)

PRONOUNCED: het-er-oh-don-toh-sawr-us

GROUP: Ornithopod dinosaur

WHERE IT LIVED: South Africa

WHEN IT LIVED: Early Jurassic Period (208 to 200 million years ago)

LENGTH: 4 feet (1.2 meters)

SPECIAL FEATURES: Three kinds of teeth – nipping teeth inside the beak at the front, tusks at the side, and grinding teeth at the back

FOOD: Plants

MAIN ENEMY: Meat-eating dinosaurs and crocodiles

DID YOU KNOW?: *Heterodontosaurus* had five-fingered hands, but two of the fingers were tiny.

It is possible that only male *Heterodontosaurus* had the long side tusks. Maybe they were used for display during the mating season, to scare away rivals. Like other ornithopods, *Heterodontosaurus* had a bird-like beak at the front of the mouth.

49

STEGOSAURUS

One of the most recognizable of the armored dinosaurs was *Stegosaurus*. It had a double row of plates down its back. These were either covered in horns and used for defense, or covered in skin and used to keep the dinosaur warm – we are not yet sure which.

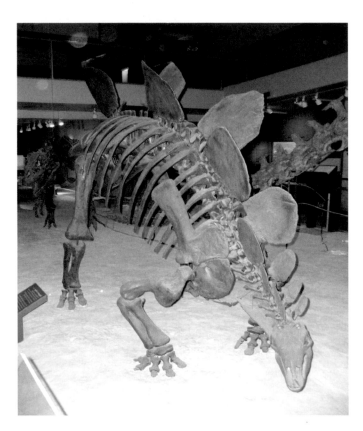

Stegosaurus may have used its plates to keep warm. When it was cold it would have stood sideways to the sun, so sunlight could warm the plates. When *Stegosaurus* was hot it could have cooled itself off by holding the plates into the wind.

ANIMAL
FACTFILE

NAME: *Stegosaurus* (roofed lizard)

PRONOUNCED: steg-oh-sawr-us

GROUP: Thyreophoran dinosaur

WHERE IT LIVED: Midwestern United States

WHEN IT LIVED: Late Jurassic Period (156 to 140 million years ago)

LENGTH: 30 feet (9 meters)

SPECIAL FEATURES: Two pairs of spikes on tail for defense

FOOD: Plants

MAIN ENEMY: Big meat-eating dinosaurs like *Allosaurus*

DID YOU KNOW?: The brain of *Stegosaurus* is so small that people used to think it must have had a second brain in its hips to control the legs and tail.

Stegosaurus probably spent most of its time on four legs. However, its hips and hind legs were very strong, showing that it could rear up on its hind legs to eat from the low branches of trees.

BRACHIOSAURUS

One of the biggest dinosaurs was *Brachiosaurus*.
It was one of the long-necked plant-eating sauropods.
There were many types of big sauropods in the Late
Jurassic Period. Some were adapted for grazing the
plants that grew close to the ground. Others, like
Brachiosaurus, were tall so they could
eat the leaves and needles
from high trees.

Brachiosaurus!
One of the
biggest land-living animals known! How on earth
could it support that great weight? In fact, the
bones of *Brachiosaurus* weren't as heavy as they look.
They were hollow, which made them extremely strong,
but lightweight at the same time.

ANIMAL
FACTFILE

NAME: *Brachiosaurus* (arm lizard)

PRONOUNCED: brack-ee-oh-sawr-us

GROUP: Sauropod dinosaur

WHERE IT LIVED: East Africa and the Midwestern United States

WHEN IT LIVED: Mid to Late Jurassic Period (160 to 145 million years ago)

LENGTH: 80 feet (24 meters)

SPECIAL FEATURES: Long neck, small head. The tail was 25 feet (8 meters) long — relatively short for a sauropod

FOOD: Leaves from trees

MAIN ENEMY: Big meat-eating dinosaurs like *Allosaurus*

DID YOU KNOW?: *Brachiosaurus* fossils have been found in both Africa and North America, showing that the two continents were close together in Late Jurassic times.

Can you picture how big *Brachiosaurus* was? This photo might help. *Brachiosaurus* was over 40 feet (12 meters) tall, about the height of a four-story building.

ALLOSAURUS

One of the biggest and fiercest of the meat-eating dinosaurs in the Late Jurassic Period was *Allosaurus*. It was big enough to hunt the biggest of the plant-eating sauropods, although, like lions and tigers today, it probably concentrated on the young, the old, and the injured.

Over 40 skeletons of *Allosaurus* have been found in a single quarry in Utah. Most of the mounted *Allosaurus* skeletons that we see in museums today have come from this site.

With the big claws on its three-fingered hands, *Allosaurus* could seize its prey. It would then have killed it with its steak-knife teeth. After it had finished eating its prey, there would have been plenty left over for smaller scavenging dinosaurs and pterosaurs.

ANIMAL
FACTFILE

NAME: *Allosaurus* (different lizard)

PRONOUNCED:
al-oh-sawr-us

GROUP: Theropod dinosaur

WHERE IT LIVED: Western United States

WHEN IT LIVED: Late Jurassic Period (156 to 145 million years ago)

LENGTH: 38 feet (11.5 meters)

SPECIAL FEATURES: The biggest land-living meat-eater of the time

FOOD: Big plant-eating dinosaurs, like *Stegosaurus* or *Brachiosaurus*

MAIN ENEMY: None

DID YOU KNOW?: *Allosaurus* weighed 5 tons — about the weight of an elephant. There were several smaller species, some weighing as little as 1 ton.

UANLONG

The most famous meat-eating dinosaur of all time must be *Tyrannosaurus. Guanlong* was an early relative. It was quite small considering the size of its relatives. But it was still a fierce hunter of smaller animals.

Most small active animals, like mammals and birds, are warm-blooded. Hair or feathers help them to control their body temperature. We think that the small meat-eating dinosaurs were active enough to have been warm blooded and so we think they probably had a feathery covering.

ANIMAL
FACTFILE

NAME: *Guanlong* (crowned dragon)

PRONOUNCED: gwan-long

GROUP: Theropod dinosaur

WHERE IT LIVED: China

WHEN IT LIVED: Late Jurassic Period (160 million years ago)

LENGTH: 10 feet (3 meters)

SPECIAL FEATURES: The earliest tyrannosaur known

FOOD: Other dinosaurs

MAIN ENEMY: Bigger meat-eating dinosaurs

DID YOU KNOW?: Until *Guanlong* was discovered, scientists thought that tyrannosaurs only lived in Cretaceous times.

Fossils show that *Guanlong* had a crest on its head. This is something unusual among the tyrannosaurs. It would have been used for signaling to other dinosaurs.

QUETZALCOATLUS

Toward the end of the Cretaceous era, the flying reptiles – the pterosaurs – became truly enormous. *Quetzalcoatlus* was among the biggest, and was the size of a small airplane. Despite its huge wingspan, it would not have weighed much more than an adult human.

Most pterosaurs lived near the sea, where they hunted for fish. *Quetzalcoatlus* was different; it lived far inland. It may have been a scavenger, feeding on the bodies of dinosaurs that had died on the open plains. It would have soared like a vulture and spotted dead animals from far away.

ANIMAL
FACTFILE

NAME: *Quetzalcoatlus* (after the ancient Mexican god, Quetzalcoatl, that took the form of a flying serpent)

PRONOUNCED: ket-sal-koh-aht-lus

GROUP: Pterosaur

WHERE IT LIVED: Texas

WHEN IT LIVED: Late Cretaceous Period (65 million years ago)

WINGSPAN: 35 feet (10.6 meters)

SPECIAL FEATURES: Broad wings, long neck, very long jaws

FOOD: Possibly carrion

MAIN ENEMY: None

DID YOU KNOW?: *Quetzalcoatlus* is one of the biggest ever flying animals. Today, the bird with the largest wingspan is the albatross, which has a wingspan of 11 feet (3.3 meters).

A complete skeleton of *Quetzalcoatlus* has never been found. We have a good idea of what it looked like from the few fossils that have been found and put together, like this one.

ELASMOSAURUS

The plesiosaurs were swimming reptiles, and most had very long necks. *Elasmosaurus* had a neck that was 25 feet (7.5 meters) long – more than half of its total length. It cruised the warm waters of the shallow sea that stretched across North America at the end of the Cretaceous Period, hunting fish that were in great supply there.

The way the vertebrae of the neck are joined together suggests that *Elasmosaurus* swam near the surface of the water and reached down to catch its prey. The long neck probably also allowed it to reach out and snatch fish, without moving its body too far or too quickly.

Elasmosaurus had tiny nostrils which were not used for breathing, but to sense prey moving in the water. To breathe, *Elasmosaurus* would have swum to the surface of the sea to take in air through its mouth.

ANIMAL
FACTFILE

NAME: *Elasmosaurus* (thin plate lizard)

PRONOUNCED: eh-laz-mo-sawr-us

GROUP: Plesiosaur

WHERE IT LIVED: Kansas

WHEN IT LIVED: Late Cretaceous Period (69 to 66 million years ago)

LENGTH: 45 feet (13 meters)

SPECIAL FEATURES: Long neck with 71 vertebrae (we humans have only 7)

FOOD: Fish

MAIN ENEMY: Big swimming reptiles like *Tylosaurus*

DID YOU KNOW?: The first scientist to study *Elasmosaurus* built the skeleton wrongly. He put the head on the tail end, thinking the short tail was the neck and the long neck was the tail.

IGUANODON

Iguanodon was one of the first dinosaurs to be discovered. Scientists studying its fossil thought that it looked like a big reptile. Most big reptiles are meat-eaters, but the teeth of this fossil showed it ate plants. The iguana, a plant-eating lizard, has teeth similar to *Iguanodon*. So the plant-eating dinosaur was named *Iguanodon* – "iguana tooth."

Scientists used to think that *Iguanodon* stood upright, resting on its tail like a kangaroo. Now they think that it usually walked on all fours, and only reached up to feed.

Iguanodon was common in northern Europe, but it had close relatives all over the world. *Muttaburrasaurus* lived in Australia, while big-nosed *Altirhinus* (right) lived in Mongolia.

ANIMAL FACTFILE

NAME: *Iguanodon* (iguana tooth)

PRONOUNCED: ig-wan-oh-don

GROUP: Ornithopod dinosaur

WHERE IT LIVED: Northern Europe

WHEN IT LIVED: Early Cretaceous Period (135 to 125 million years ago)

LENGTH: 30 feet (9 meters)

SPECIAL FEATURES: First finger had a big horny spike for defense, and for ripping trees

FOOD: Plants

MAIN ENEMY: Big meat-eating dinosaurs, like *Neovenator*

DID YOU KNOW?: *Iguanodon's* fifth finger was small and flexible, and used like a thumb.

STYGIMOLOCH

At the end of the Cretaceous Period, a group of dinosaurs called the marginocephalians developed. One group of marginocephalians was the boneheads. These goat-sized animals had a massive lump of bone on their head that they used as a battering ram. One of the strangest-looking boneheads was *Stygimoloch*.

Fossil dinosaur skulls are rare, because the delicate bones fall to pieces soon after death. The skulls of the marginocephalians are different. They were so solid that they are often found as fossils, even though the rest of the skeleton has disappeared.

ANIMAL FACTFILE

NAME: *Stygimoloch* (horned devil from the river of death)

PRONOUNCED: stig-ih-moe-lock

GROUP: Marginocephalian

WHERE IT LIVED: Canada and the mid-west of the United States

WHEN IT LIVED: Late Cretaceous Period (68 to 65 million years ago)

LENGTH: 9 feet (2.7 meters)

SPECIAL FEATURES: The stiff, straight tail was used for balance

FOOD: Plants

MAIN ENEMY: Big meat-eating dinosaurs like *Tyrannosaurus*

DID YOU KNOW?: All boneheads used their heavy heads as weapons to head-butt their rivals.

Stygimoloch had a spectacular number of horns around its skull. These would have been used to make it look bigger and fiercer than it actually was, to scare away enemies.

65

TRICERATOPS

Triceratops is one of the most recognizable of the dinosaurs. It had a huge rhinoceros-like body and a massive bony head with three horns pointing forward. It roamed the plains of North America in herds at the very end of the "Age of Dinosaurs."

Triceratops had a big beak at the front of its mouth. It used this to snip off shoots and twigs from bushes and trees. It had chopping teeth at the back of its mouth, and cheek pouches to hold its food while chewing it.

Triceratops was a ceratopsian dinosaur. There were many types of ceratopsian dinosaurs. They all looked very similar to one another, except for the number and arrangement of horns on the head. Some had a single horn on the nose, some had a pair of horns over the eyes, and some had horns on the armored shield around the neck.

ANIMAL
FACTFILE

NAME: *Triceratops* (three-horned face)

PRONOUNCED: try-sair-oh-tops

GROUP: Marginocephalian (ceratopsian group)

WHERE IT LIVED: North America

WHEN IT LIVED: Late Cretaceous Period (72 to 65 million years ago)

LENGTH: 25 feet (7.5 meters)

SPECIAL FEATURES: A solid armored shield around the neck

FOOD: Tough plants

MAIN ENEMY: Big meat-eating dinosaurs like *Tyrannosaurus*

DID YOU KNOW?: *Triceratops* was one of the last dinosaurs to develop before all dinosaurs became extinct 65 million years ago, leaving only their descendants, the birds.

67

SUCHOMIMUS

This frightening creature belongs to a group of dinosaurs called the spinosaurids. These fish eating creatures lived in the Early Cretaceous Period. *Suchomimus* might have used its claws to hook the fish out of water, throw them onto the land, and snap them up in its long jaws.

Suchomimus was a very powerful dinosaur. Its skull was crocodile-like, with a long snout and a large number of sharp teeth. These would have allowed it to grasp the slippery surface of a fish's scaly skin.

Suchomimus was a fierce predator, but even it was hunted by bigger creatures. In this picture, a gigantic crocodile lunges out of the water to attack *Suchomimus*.

ANIMAL
FACTFILE

NAME: *Suchomimus* (crocodile mimic)

PRONOUNCED: soo-cho-my-mas

GROUP: Theropod

WHERE IT LIVED: North Africa

WHEN IT LIVED: Early Cretaceous Period (110 to 100 million years ago)

LENGTH: 36 feet (11 meters)

SPECIAL FEATURES: Long narrow crocodile-like jaws

FOOD: Fish

MAIN ENEMY: A gigantic crocodile called *Sarcosuchus*

DID YOU KNOW?: The spinosaurids were a widespread group. Closely related dinosaurs have been found in England, Thailand, and Brazil.

69

UITRERAPTOR

Scientists used to think that the small, fast, meat-eating dinosaurs that looked like birds only lived in Europe, Africa, and North America. Then, in 2005, scientists found the remains of *Buitreraptor* in South America. In the Cretaceous Period, South America was an island, like Australia today. This means that the ancestors of *Buitreraptor* and the rest of the bird-like dinosaurs must have existed before the continents broke up, maybe 200 million years ago.

Scientists have not found fossilized feathers with *Buitreraptor*. They think it had feathers because its long legs and light build show that it was very active, and so probably warm-blooded. Most warm-blooded animals have fur or feathers to keep themselves warm. Relatives of *Buitreraptor* had feathers, so it is likely that *Buitreraptor* did, too.

Several skeletons of *Buitreraptor* were found in the same general area, in South America. It looks as though it was quite a common animal at the time. From the many remains, scientists have been able to build up a complete skeleton.

ANIMAL FACTFILE

NAME: *Buitreraptor* (Vulture hunter)

PRONOUNCED: bewt-re-rap-tor

GROUP: Theropod

WHERE IT LIVED: Argentina

WHEN IT LIVED: Late Cretaceous Period of the Mesozoic Era (90 million years ago)

LENGTH: 4 feet (1.2 meters), but most of this was tail and neck. The body was the size of a chicken.

SPECIAL FEATURES: A bird-like dinosaur with feathers, long legs, wing-like limbs, and a long beak-like snout. It had smaller and fewer teeth than other meat-eating dinosaurs.

FOOD: Small animals

MAIN ENEMY: Bigger meat-eaters

DID YOU KNOW?: The long, narrow jaws and small, widely-spaced teeth may mean that *Buitreraptor* probed down burrows for snakes. Scientists found fossils of snakes at the *Buitreraptor* site.

DEINONYCHUS

Is it a bird? Is it a dinosaur? In the Cretaceous Period, some of the more active meat-eating dinosaurs were so bird-like that it is difficult to decide if they were birds or dinosaurs. *Deinonychus* was one of the most bird-like.

Deinonychus did not fly – its arms were too small to support its body in flight. It had a heavy head, toothy jaws, and a long, stiff tail to balance it as it ran. These are dinosaur features rather than bird features.

The bones of *Deinonychus* were lightweight and hollow, just like a bird's. It had strong muscles for running or jumping. It was obviously a very active animal, and so it was probably warm-blooded. It is likely that *Deinonychus* had a feathery coat to keep it warm.

ANIMAL
FACTFILE

NAME: *Deinonychus* (terrible claw)

PRONOUNCED: dye-non-ik-us

GROUP: Theropod

WHERE IT LIVED: Western United States

WHEN IT LIVED: Middle Cretaceous Period (110 to 100 million years ago)

LENGTH: 10 feet (3 meters), including the long tail

SPECIAL FEATURES: Big killing claw, 5 inches (12 cm) long, on the hind foot, for slashing its prey

FOOD: Other dinosaurs

MAIN ENEMY: None

DID YOU KNOW?: The fossils of several *Deinonychus* have been found surrounding those of a big plant-eater. They may have hunted this animal in packs.

73

TYRANNOSAURUS

Since its discovery about a hundred years ago, *Tyrannosaurus* has been regarded as one of the fiercest dinosaurs that ever lived. Weighing over six tons, *Tyrannosaurus* would have been an unstoppable force once it began to attack.

Tyrannosaurus was a fearsome hunter. The remains of duckbilled dinosaurs have been found with chunks torn out of them – in the exact shape of *Tyrannosaurus'* mouth. Fossilized *Tyrannosaurus* dung has been found, full of crunched-up bone fragments from the biggest plant-eaters of the time.

Tyrannosaurus walked on two legs with its back horizontal. Its massive jaws and killing teeth were thrust forward, and its body was balanced by a heavy tail. This is how *Tyrannosaurus* moved about and became the terror of the last dinosaurs that ever existed.

ANIMAL
FACTFILE

NAME: *Tyrannosaurus* (tyrant lizard)

PRONOUNCED: tie-ran-oh-sawr-us

GROUP: Theropod

WHERE IT LIVED: Canada and the Western United States

WHEN IT LIVED: Late Cretaceous Period (85 to 65 million years ago)

LENGTH: 40 feet (12 meters)

SPECIAL FEATURES: Huge head with forward pointing eyes to help in hunting, and tiny arms

FOOD: Other dinosaurs — especially duckbills

MAIN ENEMY: None

DID YOU KNOW?: It's possible that *Tyrannosaurus* was a scavenger as well as a hunter.

MEGISTOTHERIUM

Before the emergence of modern carnivores, such as lions and bears, there was a group of predators called the creodonts. *Megistotherium* was the biggest of these, with a skull twice as long as a tiger's. It might have been the largest hunting land mammal that has ever lived.

This is the skull of a creodont. Not all creodonts were as big as *Megistotherium* – some were only the size of a weasel. But all creodonts were fierce hunters, with powerful jaws and great bone-crushing, meat-ripping teeth.

ANIMAL
FACTFILE

NAME: *Megistotherium* (the biggest beast)

PRONOUNCED: meh-jiss-toe-theer-ee-um

GROUP: Creodont mammal

WHERE IT LIVED: North Africa

WHEN IT LIVED: Mid Tertiary Period (50 to 20 million years ago)

LENGTH: 15.75 feet (4.8 meters)

SPECIAL FEATURES: The biggest meat-eating land mammal known

FOOD: Big animals like elephants

MAIN ENEMY: None

DID YOU KNOW?: Only a single complete skull of *Megistotherium* has been found, although small pieces of other skulls have been discovered.

With a head that measured about 4 feet (1.2 meters) long, and a body that must have been the size of a bison, *Megistotherium* was big enough, powerful enough and fierce enough to hunt and eat elephants!

PYROTHERIUM

For most of the Tertiary Period, South America
was separated from North America by sea.
Different mammals developed in South America
because it was an island. Some animals looked like
those that lived on other continents, but they were
not related. *Pyrotherium* looked like an elephant.

Male *Pyrotherium* may have used their
tusks and trunks to fight with one
another to decide who was going to
mate with the females.

With its tusks and trunk, *Pyrotherium* must have looked like an elephant. It may have lived like one too, digging in the ground with its tusks, and picking up food with its short trunk.

ANIMAL
FACTFILE

NAME: *Pyrotherium* (fire mammal, because its fossils were found near a volcano)

PRONOUNCED: pi-ro-theer-ee-um

GROUP: Pyrothere group of the xenungulates — the "foreign hoofed mammals"

WHERE IT LIVED: Bolivia and Argentina

WHEN IT LIVED: Mid Tertiary Period (29 to 23 million years ago)

LENGTH: 8.8 feet (2.7 meters)

SPECIAL FEATURES: Heavy animal with a trunk and tusks

FOOD: Plants

MAIN ENEMY: Big meat-eating marsupials

DID YOU KNOW?: *Pyrotherium* was such a mixture of different kinds of animal that it is difficult to tell what it is related to. It had the tusks and trunk of an elephant, teeth like a hippopotamus, and the ear bones of a hoofed mammal.

UINTATHERIUM

The *Uintatherium* may have looked like a rhinoceros, with a big heavy body and horns, but they were not related. Many rhinoceros-like mammals lived in early Tertiary times. They probably developed to take the place of horned dinosaurs like *Triceratops*, that had only just become extinct.

Uintatherium weighed something like two tons, and carried itself on massive elephant-like legs. It was probably only the males that had the 3 feet (1 meter) long tusks. They may have used them to attract or scare other animals.

Uintatherium must have looked very frightening. It had six horns on its head and a pair of sharp tusks in its upper jaw. However, it was probably a slow-witted plant-eater.

ANIMAL
FACTFILE

NAME: *Uintatherium* (mammal from the Uinta Mountains in the U.S.)

PRONOUNCED: you-in-ta-theer-ee-um

GROUP: Uintathere

WHERE IT LIVED: Utah

WHEN IT LIVED: Early Tertiary Period (40 to 35 million years ago)

LENGTH: 13 feet (4 meters)

SPECIAL FEATURES: Three pairs of horns and a pair of sharp tusks

FOOD: Plants

MAIN ENEMY: None

DID YOU KNOW?: In the 1870s two American palaeontologists, Othniel Marsh and Edward Cope, argued bitterly over who should name this animal. It was finally named *Uintatherium* by another paleontologist, Joseph Leidy, in 1872.

NDRICOTHERIUM

This massive beast is an ancient relative of the rhinoceros. Unlike modern rhinoceroses, it did not have a horn on its nose. An animal this size would not need a weapon to defend itself. It is the biggest known land mammal ever to have lived.

As can be seen from this fossil, the *Indricotherium* had two pairs of teeth at the front of the mouth. It also had two tusk-like teeth on the upper jaw that pointed downward and two on the lower jaw that pointed forward. Together they were used for scraping leaves and twigs from high branches to eat.

ANIMAL
FACTFILE

NAME: *Indricotherium* (mammal of Indrik – a monster of local legends)

PRONOUNCED: in-drik-oh-theer-ee-um

GROUP: Perissodactyl (odd-toed hoofed mammals)

WHERE IT LIVED: Pakistan

WHEN IT LIVED: Mid-Tertiary Period (20 to 30 million years ago)

LENGTH: 26.2 feet (8 meters) long, and 14.75 feet (4.5 meters) tall at the shoulder. An elephant is about 23 feet (7 meters) long and 10 feet (3 meters) tall at the shoulder

SPECIAL FEATURES: The biggest land mammal that we know of

FOOD: Leaves and twigs

MAIN ENEMY: None

DID YOU KNOW?: *Indricotherium* must have weighed about 10 tons.

Although *Indricotherium* was like a rhinoceros, it lived more like a giraffe. Its long legs, on three-toed feet, held its body high above the ground. The tall neck and the head (which was over 3 feet [1 meter] long) reached to the tops of the highest trees.

83

BASILOSAURUS

One of the earliest whales was *Basilosaurus*. Like all whales, it was a mammal. Although mammals developed on land, many of them returned to the sea at the beginning of the Tertiary Period. The giant sea reptiles had become extinct, and sea-living mammals developed to take their place.

Like the whales of today, *Basilosaurus* would have needed to come to the surface to breathe. It had nostrils at the tip of its nose, rather than a blowhole on top of its head as modern whales do.

ANIMAL
FACTFILE

NAME: *Basilosaurus* (emperor lizard)

PRONOUNCED: bass-il-oh-sawr-us

GROUP: Archaeocete whale

WHERE IT LIVED: All the oceans

WHEN IT LIVED: Early Tertiary Period (45 to 35 million years ago)

LENGTH: 60 feet (18 meters)

SPECIAL FEATURES: A long, thin and flexible body, ideal for catching fish

FOOD: Fish and cephalopods

MAIN ENEMY: Maybe sharks

DID YOU KNOW?: Although it is a mammal, *Basilosaurus* has a name like a dinosaur. This is because the first scientist to find its fossils thought that they came from a giant reptile.

This fossil shows the long, snake-like backbone of *Basilosaurus*. Over a hundred years ago, someone stuck several bones together from different skeletons and tried to pass it off as a sea serpent.

DESMOSTYLUS

This hippopotamus-like animal with strange crooked legs lived around the edge of the Pacific Ocean in mid-Tertiary times. It probably used its tusks and heavy teeth to root about on the shallow sea floor for shellfish, or perhaps it grazed on seaweeds. It was such an odd animal that scientists are not sure what it ate!

This is a fossil of *Desmostylus'* teeth. From the chemicals in its bones, scientists have worked out that it spent most of its time in water — by the shore or in river mouths.

ANIMAL
FACTFILE

NAME: *Desmostylus* (chain-tooth, after the way the back teeth are linked together)

PRONOUNCED: des-mo-sty-lus

GROUP: Desmostylid mammal

WHERE IT LIVED: Coasts of Japan and California

WHEN IT LIVED: Mid to Late Tertiary Period (14 to 19 million years ago)

LENGTH: 5.9 feet (1.8 meters)

SPECIAL FEATURES: A lumbering semi-aquatic mammal with powerful teeth

FOOD: Shellfish or seaweed

MAIN ENEMY: Sharks

DID YOU KNOW?: The nearest living relative of *Desmostylus* is the elephant.

The inwardly-turned feet of *Desmostylus* made it very clumsy while walking on land. Underwater, though, it would have been very graceful. It could walk across the sea bed as a hippopotamus does in African rivers today.

GOMPHOTHERIUM

Elephants existed for most of the Tertiary Period. They started as small pig-like animals, but soon developed into big beasts with tusks and trunks. Many types of elephants developed with different arrangements of tusks. *Gomphotherium* was an elephant with four tusks.

The tusks on the lower jaw of *Gomphotherium* made the jaw very long and spade-like. The tusks could have been used for rooting in the forest floor, or in the beds of streams and lakes looking for food.

We do not know for sure if *Gomphotherium* had a trunk because trunks are made of flesh that does not fossilize. However, the short neck shows that the head could not reach the ground, and the skull shows features similar to the trunk area of modern elephants. As a result, scientists think the *Gomphotherium* probably had a trunk.

ANIMAL FACTFILE

NAME: *Gomphotherium* (bolted mammal)

PRONOUNCED: gomp-foe-theer-ee-um

GROUP: Elephant

WHERE IT LIVED: Europe, Kenya, Pakistan, Japan, and North America

WHEN IT LIVED: Late Tertiary Period (23 to 3 million years ago)

LENGTH: 13 feet (4 meters)

SPECIAL FEATURES: Elephant with a pair of tusks on the upper jaw and another on the lower

FOOD: Plants

MAIN ENEMY: None

DID YOU KNOW?: *Gomphotherium* probably developed in Africa and then spread to the rest of the world.

DEINOTHERIUM

Modern elephants have their tusks on the upper jaw.
Deinotherium had its tusks on the lower jaw and
they turned downwards. These tusks could
have been used as picks for digging up
roots and other ground vegetation.

Deinotherium is one of largest land animals
known. It existed for almost 20 million
years – a very long time.

The early discovery of *Deinotherium* skulls on the Greek Islands may have led to the legend of the Cyclops – the one-eyed giant. The nostrils in the skull are fused into a single hole, which looks like an enormous eye socket.

ANIMAL FACTFILE

NAME: *Deinotherium* (terrible mammal)

PRONOUNCED: dy-no-theer-ee-um

GROUP: Elephant

WHERE IT LIVED: Africa and Southern Europe

WHEN IT LIVED: Late Tertiary Period (20 to 2 million years ago)

HEIGHT: 13 feet (4 meters) at the shoulders

SPECIAL FEATURES: Down-curved tusks on the lower jaw

FOOD: Plants

MAIN ENEMY: None

DID YOU KNOW?: *Deinotherium* was around at the same time as our earliest human ancestors.

AMPHICYON

Amphicyon was as big as a grizzly bear. It was one of the largest hunting animals in Middle Tertiary times. With its massive body and powerful legs it could hunt down most of the animals that were around, and kill them with its sharp dog-like teeth.

The legs of *Amphicyon* were short, and it walked on flat feet like a bear. It could not have run fast. It probably hunted its prey by ambushing it rather than running it down.

The *Amphicyon* is neither a bear nor a dog, but something in between. The amphicyonids were the main hunters of the Middle Tertiary, and ranged from the size of badgers to the size of the biggest bears.

ANIMAL FACTFILE

NAME: *Amphicyon* (nearly a dog)

PRONOUNCED: am-fee-sy-on

GROUP: Amphicyonid — the bear dogs

WHERE IT LIVED: Europe and North America

WHEN IT LIVED: Mid Tertiary Period (30 to 14 million years ago)

HEIGHT: 3 feet (1 meter)

SPECIAL FEATURES: Skeleton like that of a bear, but teeth like that of a dog

FOOD: Other animals, particularly the small horses of the time

MAIN ENEMY: None

DID YOU KNOW?: The bear-dogs took over from the creodonts in the early part of the Tertiary Period, and were then replaced by the canids (wolves, foxes, and dogs) In the later part.

93

MEGALANIA

When the first people arrived in Australia 40,000 years ago, they must have been terrified by *Megalania*. This gigantic lizard was the size of a lion. It was a fierce predator, with sharp teeth and big claws. It would have hunted by ambush, lying in wait until its prey came close, then leaping out to attack.

Megalania may have hunted in short bursts of speed. It would not have been able to run fast for long. Like other reptiles, *Megalania* could not control its body temperature, and so it would have over-heated if it tried to run too fast for too long.

Scientists have not yet found a full skeleton of *Megalania*. The individual bones that have been found suggest that it had a massive body.

ANIMAL
FACTFILE

NAME: *Megalania* (great ripper)

PRONOUNCED: meg-al-ai-nee-ah

GROUP: Varanid lizard

WHERE IT LIVED: Australia

WHEN IT LIVED: Early Quaternary Period (1.6 million to 40,000 years ago)

LENGTH: 18 feet (5.5 meters)

SPECIAL FEATURES: The biggest land lizard that has ever existed

FOOD: Meat, either from animals it caught itself, or scavenged from the bodies of those that were already dead

MAIN ENEMY: Carnivorous marsupials, such as *Thylacoleo*

DID YOU KNOW?: *Megalania* would have tackled prey up to ten times its own weight. That means that it could have hunted the biggest animals in Australia at that time.

DINORNIS

Before early people reached New Zealand, about 1,000 years ago, bats were the only mammals living there. However, there was a vast range of ground-dwelling birds known as the moa. The biggest of these was *Dinornis*. It was the largest bird to have ever lived.

When you see a moa skeleton in a museum, it often has its head held high. In life it would usually have held its head close to the ground, where the food was. It would have looked up to scan for danger.

During the Quaternary Period, New Zealand was covered in forest. *Dinornis* had a short, broad beak. It was ideal for rooting about in thick forest undergrowth to find the tastiest food.

ANIMAL FACTFILE

NAME: *Dinornis* (terrible bird)

PRONOUNCED: die-nor-nis

GROUP: Ratite — flightless birds

WHERE IT LIVED: New Zealand

WHEN IT LIVED: Throughout the Quaternary Period (1.6 million to 200 years ago)

HEIGHT: 6.5 feet (2 meters) at the mid-point of the back

SPECIAL FEATURES: Giant flightless bird with a tiny head and enormous legs

FOOD: Twigs, berries, and leaves. It also swallowed stones to help to grind up the food.

MAIN ENEMY: People, and a kind of giant eagle that lived in New Zealand

DID YOU KNOW?: There were 11 different species of moa, some only the size of a turkey. Humans hunted moas to extinction a few hundred years ago.

MEGALOCEROS

Modern moose and elk have spectacular antlers. However, these are tiny compared with the antlers of the big Ice Age deer *Megaloceros*. Each antler would have been about 5 feet (1.5 meters) – longer than you are! Only male deer had antlers. They used them to attract a mate and fight off rivals.

Megaloceros lived in many European countries, but it was particularly common in Ireland, where there were few predators and plenty of food. The antlers of *Megaloceros* are often found in Irish peat bogs. For this reason, it is also known as the Great Irish Elk.

The leader of the *Megaloceros* herd must have been a magnificent sight, watching over his herd and protecting it against other males. However, he could not guard against the hunting skills of early humans. By the end of the Ice Age, it may have been hunted to extinction.

ANIMAL
FACTFILE

NAME: *Megaloceros* (giant horn)

PRONOUNCED: meg-ah-loss-er-oss

GROUP: Artiodactyl

WHERE IT LIVED: Europe and Western Asia

WHEN IT LIVED: Mid Quaternary Period (1.5 million to 11,000 years ago)

HEIGHT: 10 feet (3 meters)

SPAN OF ANTLERS: 10.8 feet (3.3 meters). Today, the largest moose antlers have a span of about 6.5 feet (2 meters)

SPECIAL FEATURES: Enormous antlers that were shed and regrown every year

FOOD: Grass and low-growing vegetation

MAIN ENEMY: Early humans

DID YOU KNOW?: *Megaloceros* needed large amounts of minerals to grow its antlers every year. About 11,000 years ago the climate became colder and the vegetation that provided these minerals became less common. Climate change, together with hunting by early humans, led to *Megaloceros'* extinction.

Mammuthus

Probably the most familiar of the Ice Age mammals is the woolly mammoth, with its long shaggy hair and massive curved tusks. Unlike today's elephants that live in hot countries, the mammoth was adapted to the cold.

Sometimes mammoths became buried in mud when they sank into a peat bog, or when a riverbank collapsed on them. This mud later froze. As a result, we sometimes find complete frozen bodies of mammoths, thousands of years old.

ANIMAL
FACTFILE

NAME: *Mammuthus* (burrowing one)

PRONOUNCED: mam-outh-us

GROUP: Elephantidae

WHERE IT LIVED: Canada, Alaska, Siberia, and Northern Europe

WHEN IT LIVED: Late Tertiary Period to Late Quaternary Period (4.8 million years ago to 2,500 years ago)

HEIGHT: 8.8 feet (2.7 meters) at the shoulders

SPECIAL FEATURES: Adaptations to living in a cold climate

FOOD: Grasses, lichens and mosses

MAIN ENEMY: Humans

DID YOU KNOW?: Mammoths were named "burrowing one" because when their bones were first found in Siberia, the local people thought that they were the remains of animals that lived underground.

The thick hair of the mammoth protected it from the cold. The hump on its shoulders contained a food supply of fat that would see it through the harsh winters. The huge curving tusks were used as snowplows, for scraping snow away from the mosses, lichens, and grasses on which it fed.

Coelodonta

The woolly rhinoceros, *Coelodonta*, is one of the most familiar Ice Age mammals. It roamed the freezing northern plains, either on its own or in small family groups. Like the mammoth, it was well-adapted to cold conditions, even though its modern relatives live in much warmer areas.

Coelodonta had many adaptations that helped keep it warm. It was covered in shaggy hair. It also had short legs and small ears, so these parts of its body did not get so cold.

The nose of the *Coelodonta* had a bony structure to support the weight of its horn, which was made of compacted hair. Both males and females had horns. They used them to push away snow, to reach the grass underneath.

ANIMAL
FACTFILE

NAME: *Coelodonta* (hollow tooth)

PRONOUNCED: see-low-dont-ah

GROUP: Perissodactyl

WHERE IT LIVED: Northern Europe and Asia

WHEN IT LIVED: Early to Mid Quaternary Period (1.8 million to 20,000 years ago)

LENGTH: 10.8 feet (3.3 meters)

SPECIAL FEATURES: Two horns, one of which was 3 feet (1 meter) long

FOOD: Grass

MAIN ENEMY: Humans

DID YOU KNOW?: Early people hunted the woolly rhinoceros and drew pictures of it on cave walls in Central Europe.

SMILODON

The sabre-tooth cats were the main hunters of big animals during Quaternary times. A sabre is a curved sword, and that is exactly what *Smilodon*'s long front teeth were like. They could easily slash through thick skin and muscle. There were many types of sabre-tooth, and *Smilodon* was the biggest.

Smilodon's powerful jaw is obvious in this skull. The canine teeth were very long and used as killing weapons. They killed by slashing their prey, not biting it as modern cats do.

ANIMAL
FACTFILE

NAME: *Smilodon* (sabre toothed)

PRONOUNCED: smy-lo-don

GROUP: Machairodont group of the cats

WHERE IT LIVED: North America

WHEN IT LIVED: Early to Mid Quaternary Period (1.6 million to 11,000 years ago)

LENGTH: 4.9 feet (1.5 meters)

SPECIAL FEATURES: 6 inch (15 centimeters) canine teeth and strong neck muscles to drive them downward with force

FOOD: Big mammals like elephants, horses, and bison

MAIN ENEMY: None

DID YOU KNOW?: Many complete skeletons of *Smilodon* have been found in Los Angeles, U.S. The animals became stuck in the tar pits there.

Smilodon was not a fast runner. Instead, it ambushed its prey and wounded it fatally. It probably would have then waited for the injured animal to bleed to death before eating it.

GIGANTOPITHECUS

The fierce *Gigantopithecus* could rear up to a great height, and bellow loudly. It was the biggest ape that ever lived. *Gigantopithecus* made its home in the forested foothills of the mountains of China.

This picture shows a model of the jaw bone of *Gigantopithecus* (bottom) compared to the jaw bone of a gorilla (top). *Gigantopithecus* is very much bigger. All that scientists really know about *Gigantopithecus* are the size of its teeth. From the teeth, and comparisons with other related animals, scientists can put together the appearance of the whole animal.

ANIMAL
FACTFILE

NAME: *Gigantopithecus* (giant ape)

PRONOUNCED: ji-gan-toe-pith-a-kuss

GROUP: Primate mammal

WHERE IT LIVED: China

WHEN IT LIVED: Late Tertiary Period to Early Quaternary Period (13 million to 500,000 years ago)

HEIGHT: 10 feet (3 meters)

SPECIAL FEATURES: Large teeth for chewing the tough mountain vegetation

FOOD: Bamboo and other plants

MAIN ENEMY: Not known

DID YOU KNOW?: *Gigantopithecus* was first discovered in 1935, when a German paleontologist found fossil teeth for sale in a Chinese medicine shop. He realized the teeth came from a primate that had never before been identified.

There is a theory that *Gigantopithecus* is still alive. Some people believe it is the Yeti, or abominable snowman, said to live in the Himalayas.

ANIMAL FAMILIES GLOSSARY

Ammonite — a group of sea-living cephalopods common in the seas of dinosaur times. They were like squid but in coiled shells, and the shells of each species were all very different from one another. Many can be found as fossils today.

Amphicyonid — the bear-dogs. These were meat-eating mammals from the Late Tertiary Period that were related both to the bears and the dogs.

Arthropod — the invertebrates with the outside shell and jointed legs. They include the modern insects, crabs, and spiders. The shell is made of material like your fingernails.

Cephalopod — literally the "head-footed" animals. The modern types, the octopus and squid, appear to have legs branching from their faces. In prehistoric times many of them had chambered shells.

Creodont — a group of early meat-eating mammals from the Early Tertiary. Although they resembled modern wolves, weasels, and bears, they were not related to them.

Gorgonopsian — a fierce group of mammal-like reptiles, looking like a cross betweena crocodile and a sabre-toothed tiger, living mainly in Permian and early Triassic times.

Graptolite — a group of tiny sea-living animals that consisted of a string of individuals attached to a stalk. They floated in the waters of the Ordovician and Silurian seas.

Ichthyosaur — a group of sea-going reptiles. They were well-adapted to living in the sea and looked like dolphins or sharks. They had fins on the tail and back, and paddles for limbs. Ichthyosaurs were common in the Triassic and the Jurassic Periods, but died out in the Cretaceous.

Labyrinthodon — one of the groups of early amphibians, from the Carboniferous and Permian Periods. They were so-called because the enamel of the teeth was contorted like a labyrinth, or maze.

Machairodont — the group of sabre-toothed cats. Their canine teeth were very long and used as killing weapons. They killed by slashing their prey, not biting it as modern cats do.

Marginocephalian — the plant-eating dinosaur group that had ornamented heads. The ornaments were sometimes horns and neck shields, and sometimes they were domes of bone used as battering rams.

Marsupial — a major group of mammals that carry their young in pouches. Nowadays they are confined to Australia, except for the opossum of the Americas. In the Tertiary Period many of the hunting animals of South America, as well as Australia, were marsupials.

Mosasaur — a group of sea reptiles from the Late Cretaceous Period. They were very much like swimming lizards with paddles instead of feet. Indeed they were very closely related to the monitor lizards of today.

Nothosaur — a sea reptile that had long jaws for catching fish and webbed feet for swimming through water. Several kinds of nothosaur lived in the shallow waters around Europe and Asia in the Triassic Period.

Ornithopod — the plant-eating dinosaur group that usually went about on two legs. They were present throughout the Late Triassic and Jurassic Periods but it was in the later Cretaceous Period that they became really important.

Pelycosaur — the most primitive group of the mammal-like reptiles, from early Permian times. Most of them had big fins on their backs. Some were meat-eaters and others were plant-eaters.

Perissodactyl — the group of odd-toed hoofed mammals. Modern forms include the horse, the rhinoceros, and the tapir. They normally have either one or three toes on the foot. The other hoofed mammal group are the artiodactyls

— the even-toed hoofed mammals, and these include the sheep, the goats, and the deer.

Placodont — a group of swimming reptiles that fed on shellfish. Many had shells like turtles, although they were not related.

Plesiosaur — the group of swimming reptiles with paddle-shaped limbs and flat bodies. There were two types — the long-necked type and the whale-like, short-necked type. They lived throughout dinosaur times.

Primate — the group of mammals that includes the lemurs, the monkeys, the apes, and ourselves. Primates have hands and forward facing eyes.

Prosauropod — an early dinosaur group that were plant-eaters and had long necks for reaching into trees. They were the biggest animals of the Triassic and early Jurassic, but not as big as their descendants — the sauropods.

Pterosaur — the flying reptiles of the age of dinosaurs. They had broad leathery wings, supported on a long fourth finger, and were covered in hair to keep them warm.

Pyrothere — a group of xenungulates that resembled the modern elephant although they were not closely related to elephants. They lived in South America in the mid-Tertiary Period.

Ratite — the group of flightless birds. Modern types include the emu and cassowary of Australia, the ostrich of Africa, and the rhea of South America.

Rauisuchian — a group of land-living meat-eaters of the Triassic Period, closely related to the crocodiles. They were the fiercest animals of the time

Sauropod — the plant-eating dinosaur group that had huge bodies, long necks, and long tails. They were the biggest land-living animals that ever lived, and reached their peak in late Jurassic times.

Spinosaurid — a type of theropod dinosaur.

Therapsid — the most mammal-like group of the mammal-like reptiles. They were covered in fur, and had teeth like the teeth of a mammal. Some were so mammal-like that you would think they were dogs.

Theropod — the meat-eating dinosaur group. They all had the same shape — long jaws with sharp teeth, long strong hind legs, smaller front legs with clawed hands, and a small body balanced by a long tail.

Thyreophoran — the armored dinosaur group. There were two main lines. The first to develop were the plated stegosaurs, and later came the armor-covered ankylosaurs.

Trilobite — a group of common sea-living arthropods, common from Cambrian to Devonian times, that had head shields, tail shields, and the body divided into segments in between.

Tyrannosaur — one of the theropod dinosaur groups. At the end of the Cretaceous Period they were among the biggest meat-eaters of all time, but the early forms, in the late Jurassic Period, were quite small animals.

Uintathere — a group of heavy, rhinoceros-like mammals from the Early Tertiary Period. They had several pairs of horn-like structures on the head and a pair of long tusks.

Varanid — the group of lizards that include the modern monitor lizards, such as the komodo dragon. Prehistoric forms include the swimming mosasaurs from the Cretaceous Period and the lion-sized lizards that lived in Australia during the Quaternary Period

Xenungulate — a group of hoofed mammals that lived in South America during the Tertiary Period. They were not related to the hoofed mammals of the rest of the world but developed independently

GLOSSARY

Abominable Snowman — an imaginary hairy ape, said to live in the Himalayan Mountains.

Adapted — changed to survive in a particular habitat or weather conditions.

Ambushing — lying in wait out of sight, and then making a surprise attack.

Amphibian — an animal that is able to live on both land and water.

Ancestors — an early form of the animal group that lived in the past.

Blowhole — a hole at the top of a whale's head that acts like its nostril. To breathe a whale comes to the surface of the water and blows air out of the hole and breathes air in. When the whale is underwater, a flap of skin covers the hole.

Canines — strong, pointed teeth.

Carnivore — a meat-eating animal.

Carrion — the meat left over from a dead animal.

Cephalopod — an animal that lives in the sea and which has a big head and tentacles, such as an octopus.

Ceratopsian dinosaur — a type of dinosaur that had frills, spikes, and horns as protection.

Cold-blooded — animals, such as reptiles or amphibians, which rely on their environment to control their body temperature.

Colonies — groups of animals of the same kind living closely together.

Compacted hair — a batch of hair that is squashed together so tightly it becomes hard.

Continents — the world's main land masses, such as Africa and Europe.

Cunning — clever at getting what they want.

Dinosaur — large group of meat-eating or plant-eating reptiles that no longer exist.

Duckbills — a type of dinosaur that had a beak that looked like a duck's beak or bill.

Extinct — an animal group which no longer exists.

Flexible — able to twist and turn easily.

Fossils — the remains of a prehistoric plant or animal that has been buried for a long time and becomes hardened in rock.

Fossilized — to turn into a fossil.

Grinding teeth — these are teeth used to chew food.

Ice Age — a period of time when the Earth was covered in ice.

Incisors — sharp-edged front teeth in the upper and lower jaws.

Hollow bones — bones that have a space inside them so that they are not solid. Hollow bones are much lighter than solid bones.

Lagoons — shallow ponds joined to seas or lakes.

Lichens — a type of plant-like moss.

Mammal — a warm-blooded animal which is covered in hair. The female gives birth to live young and produces milk from her own body to feed them.

Marsupials — an animal such as a kangaroo, which has a pouch on the front of its body in which it carries its young.

Meat-shearing teeth — special teeth that are used to cut or slice the flesh from bones.

Minerals — found in food and help to keep the body working well.

Molars — special teeth used for grinding food.

Moose — a type of deer from North America.

Oases — green areas in a desert. They contain water

and plant life.

Open plains — wide spaces without trees.

Organic matter — really tiny animal or plant life.

Ornithopod — a type of plant-eating dinosaur.

Paleontologist — a scientist who studies fossils.

Paleozoic Era — the period when life first appeared on Earth.

Peat bogs — a type of ground that is damp and covered in moss.

Plesiosaur — a reptile which lived in the sea.

Pouches — the pockets on the front of a marsupial's body.

Predators — animals that hunt and kill other animals for food.

Prehistory — a time before humans.

Prey — animals that are hunted by other animals as food.

Primitive — a very early stage in the development of a species.

Prosauropod — late Triassic Period ancestors of long-necked, plant-eating dinosaurs.

Quarry — a place where stones are dug up for building.

Reefs — ridges of rock, sand, or coral near the surface of the sea.

Reptiles — cold-blooded, crawling, or creeping animals with a backbone.

Reptilian — animals that look like a reptile.

River mouth — the place where a river flows into the sea.

Rock paintings — drawings made by our early ancestors millions of years ago .

Sauropod — a large plant-eating dinosaur.

Scavenger — an animal that feeds off food other animals have hunted.

Segments — divided into separate parts.

Semi-aquatic — animals which spend a lot of time in water but which need air to breathe, for example, turtles, otters, and frogs.

Serrated — having a jagged edge like a saw.

Snout — an animal's nose.

Soared — flew high in the sky.

Species — a group of animals which all look like each other.

Spine — the backbone of an animal.

Streamlined — a smooth, bullet-shaped body that makes it easy for the animal to move through air or water.

Tar pits — an area where thick, black, sticky liquid just under the ground bubbles up to the top.

Trilobite — an early type of sea animal that no longer exists.

Tropical — a place that is close to the equator and which has a hot, wet climate.

Tropics — hot countries that are close to the equator.

Tusk — a long pointed tooth which grows outside of an animal's mouth.

Tyrannosaur — a type of large meat-eating dinosaur.

Vertebrae — small bones that form the spine.

Warm-blooded — animals, such as small mammals, which always have the same body temperature.

Well-preserved fossil — a fossil which is in good condition.

Wing membrane — a thin sheet of skin attached to bone, which forms a wing.

Wingspan — the length of a bird's wings, from the tip of one to the tip of the other.

INDEX